Children's Songs from Afghanistan
Qu Qu Qu Barg-e-Chinaar

To the children of Afghanistan.
May their hearts forever be filled with song.

قو قو قو، برگ چنار

سرود های مشهور اطفال افغانستان

NATIONAL GEOGRAPHIC

Washington, D.C.

Musical arrangements and compositions for:
"Alphabet Song," "The Book," "Grandmother Swings Me," "Song of Saalang," and "Star" reproduced courtesy of Vaheed Kaacemy.

Credits:
Songbook Artwork, Design, and Layout by *Arsalan Lutfi, TriVision Studios*
Cover Illustration by *Susan Fisher*
Author photo, courtesy *Priscilla Harmel*
Page 4, top left, courtesy *Jim Soules*
Page 4, bottom left and top right, courtesy *Louise M. Pascale*
Page 7, photo courtesy *Hassibullah Roshan*
Pages 5-8, artwork created by Afghan children for the 1968 Songbook

National Geographic Society
1145 17th Street N.W., Washington, D.C. 20036-4688 U.S.A.

Visit us online at **www.nationalgeographic.com/books**
For librarians and teachers: **www.ngchildrensbooks.com**
More for kids from National Geographic: **kids.nationalgeographic.com**

For information about special discounts for bulk purchases, please contact
National Geographic Books Special Sales: ngspecsales@ngs.org

For rights or permissions inquiries, please contact
National Geographic Books Subsidiary Rights: ngbookrights@ngs.org

Printed in the United States of America

فهرست آهنگها
Table of Contents

	5	Introduction
الفبا	8	Alphabet Song
علی بابا	9	Ali Baba
سلام سلام	10	Hello, Hello
قصهٔ نان	11	Bread Story
توپک خالخالی	12	Polka Dot Ball
دبودی تال	13	Grandmother Swings Me
گیزگیز دان	14	Gheej Gheej Don
گنجشکک طلایی	15	Little Golden Bird
قوقوقو برگ چنار	16	Coo Coo Coo Maple Leaf
غچی	17	Little Red Bird
بابه زنجیر باف	18	Old Man Who Braids Chains
ترانهٔ سالنگ	19	Song of Saalang
ترانهٔ بهار	20	Song of Spring
کتاب	21	The Book
ستاره	22	Star
مردم افغان	23	Afghan People
	24	Additional Notes about Songs
	25	Transliteration of Songs
	30	Map of Afghanistan with Provinces
	31	Special Thanks

Louise Pascale with children–Kabul, Afghanistan, 1967

Ustad Ghulam Hussein with children–Kabul, Afghanistan, 1945

Vaheed Kaacemy with children–Toronto, Canada, 2006

Maestro Ghulam Hussein *(top right)* is considered "The Father of Music" in Afghanistan. He is held in high esteem for his progressive thinking about the role of music in culture. The original songbook, printed in 1968, was dedicated to him.

Louise Pascale *(top left)*, the author, lived in Afghanistan for two years in the late 1960s. Making music with children in Kabul inspired her to return the songs to Afghanistan some 40 years later.

Vaheed Kaacemy, composer and musician *(bottom left)*, generously worked with Afghan children in Toronto to record the CD that accompanies this book.

مقدمه
Introduction

This Afghan children's songbook had its beginnings in 1966, when I joined the United States Peace Corps as a volunteer in Kabul, Afghanistan. Afghanistan was, at that time, a peaceful country in which there was a feeling of safety and well-being, despite the poverty and lack of resources.

Having an interest in music and education, I soon became aware that there were no music books in the elementary schools, so together with an Afghan musician, Hafizullah Khial, a Pashtu poet, Selaab, and an elementary teacher, Hamida Hamid, I collected songs and put together a small songbook, which I then took to the local schools. I taught the children the songs and had the students create illustrations. (The original drawings are shown throughout this Introduction.)

In 1968, at the end of my Peace Corps service, the songbook was published by the Kabul Press and dedicated to Ustad Ghulam Hussein, a highly respected Afghan folk musician (1878-1957), who was well known by all Afghans for his passionate commitment to making music accessible to everyone, particularly children.

Almost four decades later, now a professor in the Creative Arts in Learning Division of Lesley University, Cambridge, Massachusetts, I discovered my worn and faded copy of that songbook in my bookcase. Keenly aware that Afghanistan had suffered almost two decades of war and the systematic eradication of all music under the Taliban, I feared that my copy of the songbook was perhaps the only one left in existence and that these children's songs could be lost forever. I made a commitment at that moment to return the songs to the children of Afghanistan. With this goal in mind, I founded the Afghan Children's Songbook Project.

Working with Arsalan Lutfi of TriVision Studios, and with support from Mrs. Shamim Jawad and her Ayenda Foundation and the National Geographic Society, I updated and reformatted the songbook and added a CD of children singing the songs. I was fortunate to find a well-known and respected Afghan-Canadian musician, Vaheed Kaacemy, who helped arrange, rehearse, and record the songs with Afghan-Canadian children. He also researched the origin of each song, something I had not done for the original songbook. The songbook includes songs in Dari and Pashtu, the two official Afghan languages, as well as one song each in Hazaragi and Uzbek, two other major Afghan ethnic dialects.

The project came to fruition with the publication in 2007 of *Qu Qu Qu Barg-e-Chinaar: Children's Songs from Afghanistan*, produced specifically for distribution in Afghanistan. In March 2007, the first printing of 3,000 songbook packages was distributed to elementary schools across the country with assistance from the Ayenda Foundation, Mercy Corps/Afghanistan, Save the Children, and other NGOs interested in supporting education efforts in Afghanistan. Since then, as a result of many hours of tireless work by individuals and organizations, over 10,000 copies have been printed and delivered to children across Afghanistan.

Afghan children have very few books available to them, so *Qu Qu Qu Barg-e-Chinaar* was designed to be an extremely valuable and fundamental resource. It not only provides the children with an essential connection to their culture, but it has been designed to serve as a reading book as well, so it includes colorful illustrations and easy-to-read text. The impact of returning this music to Afghan children and their families cannot be underestimated.

After the Afghan edition of the songbook was published in 2007, I created this English edition so that music specialists and classroom teachers in English-speaking countries, as well as expatriate Afghans around the world, could learn and share the songs. In consultation with members of the Afghan community, I decided to include English translations that capture the poetry and meaning of the lyrics but do not necessarily fit perfectly with the melody. I encourage you to learn to sing the songs in their original languages, using the CD and the transliterations found at the back of the book, then use the translations to help you understand what you are singing.

Translating these songs with the care and respect they deserve was no easy task, and I want to express my immeasurable gratitude to Shamim Jawad, Arsalan Lutfi, Tabasum Lutfi, and Margaret Mills for their expertise, diligence, and abundance of support with this endeavor.

We worked hard to keep the translations true to the original lyrics in order to give the reader a sense of the wonderful lyrical poetry that is typically found in Afghan music, so at times, we chose not to use the literal translation. An example of this occurs in the "Song of Saalang." The last two lines translate literally to "My country home / I wish your name will be always shining for all life." In order to have the lyrics be more representative of the traditional poetic feeling, we changed that to "My homeland, may your name be bright/ As long as the world goes on."

I hope you enjoy this book and CD and will share it with those you love. By reading the lyrics and listening to the music, you are participating in the preservation and celebration of a rich and wonderful culture.

For more information, to support the Afghan Children's Songbook Project, or to order a copy of the original edition of *Qu Qu Qu Barg-e-Chinaar*, go to www.facone.org or call 1-781-662-7475. All net proceeds from sales go to sustain the Afghan Children's Songbook Project.

To donate a songbook to a child in Afghanistan, please visit http://nationalgeographic.com/afghanchildrensfund.

Children at the Small Heaven Orphanage, Kabul, Afghanistan, 2008, singing from *Qu Qu Qu Barg-e-Chinaar.*

الفبا
Alphabet Song

Afghan children delight in singing this Dari alphabet song.
Each syllable represents a letter in the Dari alphabet.

Aa Alef Bay Pay Tay
Say Jeem Chay Hay Khay

Aa Alef Bay Pay Tay
Say Jeem Chay Hay Khay

Aa Alef Bay Pay Tay
Say Jeem Chay Hay Khay

Aa Alef Bay Pay Tay
Say Jeem Chay Hay Khay

Daal Zaal Ray Zay Jhay Seen Sheen Swaat
Zwaat Toy Zoy Aine Ghine

Fay Qhaaf Kaaf Ghaaf Laam Meem Noon Wow
Fay Qhaaf Kaaf Ghaaf Laam Meem Noon Wow

Noon Wow Hay-gerdak Yaa
Noon Wow Hay-gerdak Yaa

ا ب پ ت
ج ج ح خ

آ ا ب پ ت
ث ج ج ح خ

آ ا ب پ ت
ث ج ج ح خ

آ ا ب پ ت
ث ج ج ح خ

د ذ ر ز ژ س
ش ص ض ط ظ ع غ

ف ق ک گ
و ن م ل

ف ق ک گ
و ن م ل

ن و ه ی
ی ه و ن

8

علی بابا

Ali Baba

This lively Dari song describes all the animals in Ali Baba's garden.

Ali Baba goes to the garden
In this garden, he has a goat
"Bah Bah Bah" - says the goat
Tell me now, what else does he have?

Ali Baba goes to the garden
In this garden, he has a cat
"Meow, meow, meow" - says the cat
Tell me now, what else does he have?

Ali Baba goes to the garden
In this garden, he has a dog
"Ghow, ghow, ghow" - says the dog
Tell me now, what else does he have?

Ali Baba goes to the garden
In this garden, he has a duck
"Qekh, Qekh, Qekh" - says the duck
Tell me now, what else does he have?

Ali Baba goes to the garden
In this garden, he has a rabbit
"Mm, mm, mm" - says the rabbit
Because he doesn't have a voice.

علی با با باغ میروه   درین باغ یک بره داره
بع بع بع میکنه
بگو دیگه چه داره

علی با با باغ میروه   درین باغ یک پشک داره
میو میو میو میکنه
بگو دیگه چه داره

علی با با باغ میروه   درین باغ یک سگک داره
غو غو غو میکنه
بگو دیگه چه داره

علی با با باغ میروه   درین باغ مرغابی داره
قغ قغ قغ میکنه
بگو دیگه چه داره

علی با با باغ میروه   درین باغ یک خرگوش داره
ام ام ام میکنه
زیرا آواز نداره

A - li Baa-ba baagh may-row - a   Da-reen baagh yak ba-ra daa -

ra   Bah bah bah   me - ko - na   Bo-go de-ga chi daa - ra

9

سلام سلام

Hello, Hello

The importance of family is the message of this Hazaragi song.

Hello, hello Aapa ju!
Hello, hello Aata ju!
Aata ju is my dear father
Aapa ju is my dear mother
Hello, hello Aapa ju!
Hello, hello Aata ju!

I love my grandfather
I love my grandmother
When my grandfather goes to the bazaar
He takes me with him

Hello, hello grandfather!
Hello, hello grandmother!
I love my dear sister
I love my dear brother
Every day, my brother
takes me to school with him

Hello, hello Aapa ju!
Hello, hello Aata ju!

سلام سلام آته جو   سلام سلام آپه جو
آپه جو مادر جانی   آته جو پدر جانی
سلام سلام آته جو   سلام سلام آپه جو

آجه جوره دوست درم   بابه جوره دوست درم
مره قت خو موبره   بابه جو بازار موره

سلام سلام آجه جو   سلام سلام بابه جو
بیرارجانه دوست درم   خوارجانه دوست درم
قت خو مکتب موبره   بیرارجو هرروز مره

سلام سلام آته جو   سلام سلام آپه جو

Sa - laam sa - laam aa - pa jo   Sa - laam sa - laam aa - ta jo

قصهٔ نان
Bread Story

This traditional Dari rhythmic chant vividly
describes the importance of bread in Afghan culture.

I ran and ran
Until I reached the mountaintop.
I saw two ladies.

One gave me water. One gave me bread.
I ate the bread myself.
I gave the water to the earth.

The earth gave me wheat.
I gave the wheat to the mill.

The mill gave me flour.
I gave the flour to the dough maker.

The dough maker gave me dough.
I gave the dough to the baker.

The baker gave me bread.
I gave the bread to the Mullah [religious teacher].

The Mullah gave me the Book [The Qu'ran].
I read his Book.
God gave me faith.

دویدم دویدم
سرکوهی رسیدم
دو تا خانمه دیدم

یکیش مره او داد
یکیش مره نان داد

نانه خودم خوردم
اوه به زمین دادم

زمین مره گندم داد
گندمه به آسیا دادم

آسیا مره آرد داد
آرده به تغار دادم

تغار مره خمیر داد
خمیره به نانوا دادم

نانوا مره نان داد
نانه به ملا دادم

ملا مره کتاب داد
کتابشه خواندم
خدا مره ایمان داد

11

توپک خالخالی
Polka Dot Ball

This playful Dari song is about a favorite toy.

My ball has colorful dots
It is round and beautiful and has flower designs
(Repeat)

When I bounce it on the ground, it bounces back
Because it is hollow inside
(Repeat)

My dear little ball,
come right back to me
My dear ball, you stay here,
If you're going, wait, I'll go with you.
Ha ha ha!

توپک من خالخالیست
گرد و قشنگ گل گلیست

توپک من خال خالیست
گرد و قشنگ گل گلیست

زنم زمین میره بالا
چون که میانش خالیست

زنم زمین میره بالا
چون که میانش خالیست

توپ عزیزک من
بیا به پیشک من

توپ عزیزم تو باش
میری باش با تو میرم

ها ها ها

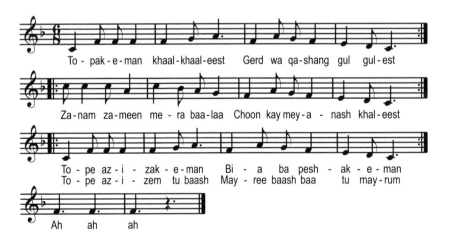

To - pak - e - man khaal - khaal - eest   Gerd wa qa - shang gul   gul - est

Za - nam za - meen me - ra baa - laa   Choon kay mey - a - nash khal - eest

To - pe az - i - zak - e - man   Bi - a ba pesh - ak - e - man
To - pe az - i - zem tu baash   May - ree baash baa   tu may - rum

Ah   ah   ah

دبودی تال

Grandmother Swings Me

Grandmothers and mothers hold a special place in this sweet Pashtu song.

Grandmother, grandmother push my swing

Push my swing high in the air

If I get cold on the swing

I know the warmth of my mother's arms will keep me warm.

بودی بودی تال راکه

تال دی په مثال راکه

تال دی په مثال راکه

تال کی به زنگیزمه

دمورغیز کی تو دیزمه

دمورغیز کی تودیزمه

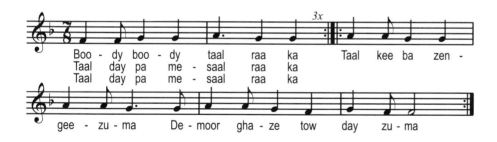

Boo - dy boo - dy taal raa ka   Taal kee ba zen -

Taal day pa me - saal raa ka

Taal day pa me - saal raa ka

gee - zu - ma   De - moor gha - ze tow day zu - ma

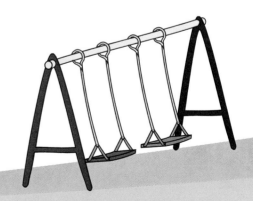

گیژگیژدان

Gheej Gheej Don

This is a catchy Uzbek children's song.

The bird sings on the rooftop
Munching on the leaf of the willow
The willow leaf is bitter,
and the heart of a beloved is aching too

Gheej Gheej Don
Oh Gheej Gheej Don
Abdul Qader Ka-mj-daan
(Chorus)*

He went out to pick pistachios
Hoping to see Jamaal (the moon-faced beauty)
"Oh Jamaal, are you home?"
"Are you sitting in your beautiful yurt?"**

(Chorus)

تامده چمچق سیری ده   تال برگینی چینی ده
تامده چمچق سیری ده   تال برگینه چینی ده
تال برگی اچیق ایکن   یوره که سنچق ایکن

گیژگیژدان   اله گیژگیژدان

عبد القادر کمژدان

چیقدم پسته تیرگنی   آی جمالنی کورگنی
چیقدم پسته تیرگنی   آی جمالنی کورگنی
آی جمال اویده سیزمه   آق اوی نینگ تورده سیزمه

گیژگیژدان   اله گیژگیژدان

عبد القادر کمژدان

* The Chorus is a bird song.
** A yurt is an Uzbek domed dwelling.

Taam-dah chem-cheq see-ry dah   Taal bar-geen-y cheen-y dah

Taal bar-gee a-cheeq ai-kaan   Yow-rah kay sin-cheq ai-kaan

Gheej gheej daan Al-la gheej gheej daan   Ab-dul Qa-der ka-mj daan

گنجشکک طلایی
Little Golden Bird

Excitement abounds with the arrival of the bride in this traditional Dari song.

The stream of water falls
The smell of pilau [pilaf] fills the air
Sweep the house, for the new bride nears!

Little golden bird, you are yellow, white, and black
You fly here and there
And take dust and dirt everywhere.
(Repeat)

The stream of water falls
The smell of pilau fills the air
Sweep the house, for the new bride nears!

Little golden bird fleeing fast, taking flight
Landing on top of the tree.

Little golden bird, you are yellow, white, and black.
(Repeat)

از بالا او میایه
خانه ره جارو کنین

گنجشکک طلایی
ایسو اوسو میپری

گنجشکک طلایی
ایسو اوسو میپری

از بالا او میایه
خانه ره جارو کنین

گنجشکک پای گریز

گنجشکک طلایی
گنجشکک طلایی

بوی پلو میایه
عروس نو میایه

زرد و سفید و سیایی
خس و خاشاک میبری

زرد و سفید و سیایی
خس و خاشاک میبری

بوی پلو میایه
عروس نو میایه

سر درخت زده خیز

زرد و سفید و سیایی
زرد و سفید و سیایی

Az baa-laa ow mey-aa__ya   Bo-oy pa-low mey-aa__ya
Khaa-na ra jaa-roo ku-nane   Aa-ros-e-now mey-aa__ya

Gun-jesh-kak-e-Tell-aa-yee   Zard o saf-aid o sia-yee
Ee-so oo-so may pa-ri   Khas o kha-shak may ba-ri

Gun-jesh-kak-e-Tell-aa-yee   Zard o saf-aid o sia-yee
Ee-so oo-so may par-i   Khas o kha-shak may bar-i

قو قو قو برگ چنار

Coo Coo Coo Maple Leaf

The title song of this book is a very old Dari chant and one that has delighted children over the ages.

Coo coo coo maple leaf
We girls are sitting in a row
Picking out seeds from the pomegranates

I wish I were a dove
Flying high in the sky
Drinking the water of Zam Zam [sacred water of Mecca]*
And picking up grains of sand from the riverbanks

But now I hear the lion's loud roar
The (mean old) lion said "Ouch! Ouch!"
And I said "Pain and misfortune on you!" *

قو قو قو برگ چنار
دخترا شیشته قطار
میچینن دانه انار

کاش که کفتر میبودم
ده هوا پر میزدم
او زمزم میخوردم
ریگ دریا میچیندم

شیرگفت الا الا
مه گفتم درد و بلا

* "Dard-o-balaa" is a common Dari expression used in two different contexts. It can be used as an unkind or as an empathetic gesture. Here, it is used as an unkind gesture.

Qu - Qu - Qu Barg - e - Chin - aar   Kaash kay kaf -
Dukh - tar - aa sheesh - ta qat - aar   Da ha - wa
Mee - chee - nan daan - e - an - aar   Ow - e - zam -
                                         Raig - e - dar -

tar may - boo - dum   Share_ guft al - laa al - laa
par may - za - dum   Ma guf - tum dard wa ba - laa
zam may - khor - dum
ya mee - chen - dum

16

غچی غچی

Little Red Bird

The coming of spring is announced by the red bird in this Dari song.

Little red bird, springtime is here	وقت گل انار شد	غچی غچی بهار شد
Pomegranate flower time is here	وقت گل انار شد	غچی غچی بهار شد
(Repeat)		
	تخمه زیر بال کو	تخم بتی زود زود
Lay your eggs. Hurry! Be quick!	بتی یکیشه به مه	هر وقت چوچه دادی
Tuck them under your wings	تخمه زیر بال کو	تخم بتی زود زود
When you hatch your little ones	بتی یکیشه به مه	هر وقت چوچه دادی
Give me one quick!		
(Repeat)		
	وقت گل انار شد	غچی غچی بهار شد
Little red bird, springtime is here	وقت گل انار شد	غچی غچی بهار شد
Pomegranate flower time is here		
(Repeat)	قا صد بهار اس	غچی گک هوشیار اس
	قا صد بهار اس	غچی گک هوشیار اس
Dear little red bird, you're so clever		
You're spring's messenger	وقت گل انار شد	غچی غچی بهار شد
(Repeat)		
	تخمه زیر بال کو	تخم بتی زود زود
Little red bird, springtime is here	تخمه زیر بال کو	تخم بتی زود زود
Pomegranate flower time is here	بتی یکیشه به مه	هر وقت چوچه دادی
Lay your eggs. Hurry! Be quick!	وقت گل انار شد	غچی غچی بهار شد
Tuck them under your wings		
(Repeat)		

When you hatch your little ones
Give me one chick

Little red bird, springtime is here
Pomegranate flower time is here

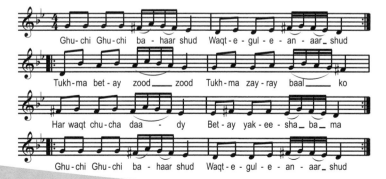

Ghu-chi Ghu-chi ba-haar shud Waqt-e-gul-e-an-aar-shud

Tukh-ma bet-ay zood___ zood Tukh-ma zay-ray baal___ ko

Har waqt chu-cha daa-___dy Bet-ay yak-ee-sha__ ba ma

Ghu-chi Ghu-chi ba-haar shud Waqt-e-gul-e-an-aar-shud

17

بابه زنجیر باف
Old Man Who Braids Chains

This Dari call-and-response chant is played as a game,
with the children asking Baba questions and Baba responding.

English call	English response	Dari response	Dari call
Baba Baba	Yes	بلی	بابه بابه
Did you braid the chains?	Yes	بلی	زنجیرا ره بافتی ؟
Did you throw them behind the castle?	Yes	بلی	پشت قلا انداختی ؟
Shall I go the Dhol* way,			از رای دول برم یا از رای سرنی؟
Or the Surnai** way?	Go the Surnai way	از رای سرنی	
Su, Su, Sur, Sur, Sur	Sur Sur Sur	سر سر سر	س س سر سر سر
Su, Su, Sur, Sur, Sur	Sur Sur Sur	سر سر سر	س س سر سر سر
Baba Baba	Yes	بلی	بابه بابه
Did you braid the chains?	Yes	بلی	زنجیراره بافتی ؟
Did you throw them behind the castle?	Yes	بلی	پشت قلا انداختی ؟
Shall I go the Dhol way,			از رای دول برم یا از رای سرنی؟
Or the Surnai way?	Go the Dhol way	از رای دول	
Dum, dum, dum, dum, dum, dum	Dum Dum Dum	دم دم دم	دم دم دم
Dum, dum, dum, dum, dum, dum		دم دم دم	دم دم دم

* Dhol is a two-sided drum.
** Surnai is a double-reeded oboe-type instrument.

ترانهٔ سالنگ
Song of Saalang

The splendor of the Saalang River Valley is described in this Dari song.

Saalang has rivers and mountains
and rushing waterfalls
Fields of flowers are everywhere

Birds are white, red, yellow, and green
and fill every branch and every tree
My homeland, may your name be bright
As long as this world goes on

Saalang is full of fruits and berries of every color
and rushing rivers
Fish are dancing joyously in the river
Fish are abundant
My homeland, may your name be bright
As long as this world goes on

(Repeat)

سالنگ کوه و دریا داره   دریا خروشان است
هر سو گلستان است
گنجشک ها سفید و سرخ و زرد و سبز پران است
بر شاخساران است
میهن نام تو روشن بود تا این جهان است
تا این جهان است

سالنگ میوه داره رنگ رنگ توتش فراوان است
دریا خروشان است
شیر ماهی به دریا مست مستان رقص رقصان است
ماهی فراوان است
میهن نام تو روشن بود تا این جهان است
تا این جهان است

سالنگ کوه و دریا داره   دریا خروشان است
هر سو گلستان است
گنجشک ها سفید و سرخ و زرد و سبز پران است
برشاخساران است
میهن نام تو روشن بود تا این جهان است
تا این جهان است

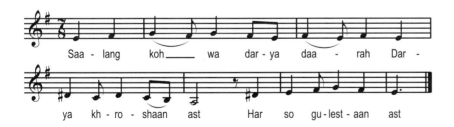

ترانهٔ بهار
Song of Spring

Springtime in Afghanistan comes to life in this Dari song.

مژده که آمد بهار   سبزه و گل بیشمار

آب فراوان به باغ   گشته روان هر کنار

غچی و پروانه شد   زنده به بوی بهار

بلبل آبی کند   غلغله در جویبار

کرده شگوفه بباغ   درخت سیب و انار

کرده شگوفه بباغ   درخت سیب و انار

بر لب آب روان   سایه بید و چنار

کو کو زنان فاخته   نشسته بر شاخسار

به شاخ سرو بلند   ناله کند زار زار

زخانه مور و ملخ   گشته روان سوی کار

تو هم بدو پشت کار   ای پسر هوشیار

تو هم بدو پشت کار   ای پسر هوشیار

Good news! Spring has come!
The grass and flowers are growing profusely
Water is flowing freely in the garden
Water is running everywhere
Birds and butterflies return
Alive with the fragrance of spring

The blue nightingale sings his song
by the waterside
The apple and pomegranate trees
have bloomed in the garden

Beside the flowing water
In the shadow of willow and maple leaf trees,
The ring dove calls "coo, coo"
Sitting on the thicket
From the branches of a tall cypress
It sings its melancholy coo, coo, coo

The ants and grasshopper leave their homes
and busily go to work

You, too, run off to work
My clever boy!
(Repeat)

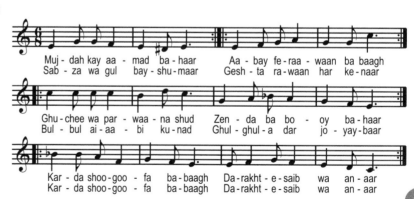

Muj - dah kay aa - mad ba - haar   Aa - bay fe - raa - waan ba baagh
Sab - za wa gul   bay-shu-maar   Gesh - ta ra-waan har ke-naar

Ghu - chee wa par - waa - na shud   Zen - da ba bo - oy ba-haar
Bul - bul ai-aa - bi ku-nad   Ghul-ghul-a dar jo - yay-baar

Kar - da shoo-goo - fa ba-baagh   Da-rakht - e -saib wa an - aar
Kar - da shoo-goo - fa ba-baagh   Da-rakht - e -saib wa an - aar

کتاب
The Book

Books are celebrated and respected in this Dari song.

I'm a friend of children
I am beautiful and eloquent
I have lots of words
Hidden within my heart

Open my heart, open my treasure-house
So I can tell you my secrets,
Tell you a hundred stories

I am a friend of children
I'm beautiful and eloquent
I have lots of words
Hidden within my heart

I'll tell you sweet stories, ancient wisdom,
Tell you tales and sing you songs.

Everyone who pays attention to me
Learns to speak beautifully and well
Through me you will gain knowledge and wisdom
Become my close friend,
and you will always have company

I am a friend of children
I am beautiful and eloquent
I have lots of words
Hidden within my heart

من دوست طفلکانم
دارم سخن فراوان

بگشا تو سینه ام را
تا با تو راز گویم

من دوست طفلکانم
دارم سخن فراوان

از قصه های شیرین
گویم به تو فسانه

هر کس که نکته دان شد
او همنشین من بود

من دوست طفلکانم
دارم سخن فراوان

زیبا و خوش بیانم
دربین سینه پنهان

واکن خزینه ام را
صد قصه باز گویم

زیبا و خوش بیانم
در بین سینه پنهان

زیبا و خوش بیان شد
دوست و قرین من بود

زیبا و خوش بیانم
در بین سینه پنهان

21

ستاره
Star

This lovely Dari song tells of the stars in the night sky.

Little star, little star, twinkling little star
Every night, it tells us a story
of the starlight sky.

ستاره جان ستاره جان چشمک زنان ستاره جان
هر شب به ما قصه میگه از آسمان ستاره جان

Rose and Lily are friends with Iris and Aquila.
Eglantine and Violet are sisters with Jasmine.

گلاب و نیلوفر رفیق سوسن و نسرین میشن
نسترن و بنفشه هم خواهر یاسمین میشن

When night falls, all the seven sisters [the constellation Pleiades]
Come out like blossoms on a bush,
and rise to the high Heaven, becoming bright as Venus.

شب که میشه هر هفت شان از گل بته پایین میشن
میرن ده آسمان بالا ستاره پروین میشن

Little star, little star, twinkling little star
Every night, it tells us a story
of the starlit sky.

ستاره جان ستاره جان چشمک زنان ستاره جان
هرشب به ما قصه میگه از آسمان ستاره جان

The moths love the star Libra.
The little lambs love the "herding" star [Venus],
The nightingale stars [in Hyades star cluster] are friends of the boys,
And the little girl loves the Pleiades.

ستاره تر از و ره شب پرکها دوست میدارن
ستاره چوپانه هم بره گک ها دوست میدارن

Little star, little star, twinkling little star
Every night, it tells us a story
of the starlit sky.

ستاره های بلبلی دوست و رفیق بچه هاست
ستاره پروینه هم دخترک ها دوست میدارن

ستاره جان ستاره جان چشمک زنان ستاره جان
هر شب به ما قصه میگه از آسمان ستاره جان

مردم افغان

Afghan People

Afghans and the majestic country of Afghanistan are honored in this popular Dari song.

We are Afghan people
We are Afghans of the mountains

ما مردم افغانیم
افغان کوهستانیم

We are Afghan people
We are Afghans of the mountains

ما مردم افغانیم
افغان کوهستانیم

We have one stance and one way
We have one faith and one hope

یک کیش و یک آیینیم
یک دین و یک آرمانیم

We have one stance and one way
We have one faith and one hope

یک کیش و یک آیینیم
یک دین و یک آرمانیم

We are Afghan people
We are Afghans of the mountains

ما مردم افغانیم
افغان کوهستانیم

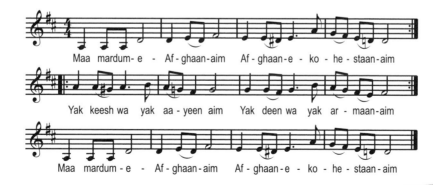

Additional Notes about Songs

Alphabet Song
Recently composed by Vaheed Kaacemy for young Afghan children, this is the first alphabet song written for the Dari alphabet. The song is based on the ancient music of Heart and the rhythm of Maqaam-e-Chargah.

Ali Baba
This playful little song, similar to the American folksong "Old McDonald Had a Farm" takes children through a garden filled with delightful animals. This melody is believed to have originated in Turkey.

Hello, Hello
Originating from the Bamian Province, this song beautifully illustrates the warmth and compassion the Hazaragi people have for their families.

Bread Story
In this ancient chant, written as a sequential story, a loaf of bread begins as a simple grain of wheat in the earth and ends up becoming an important gift for the Mullah.

Polka Dot Ball
For many, many years, Afghan children have enjoyed singing this playful song about the pretty polka dot ball.

Grandmother Swings Me
Grandmother Swings Me, arranged by Vaheed Kaacemy and based on traditional Pashtu melody and lyrics, describes the warmth and comfort a child often finds in the arms of his/her mother or grandmother.

Gheej Gheej Don
The music and lyrics of this traditional Uzbek song originate from the northern Faryab Province near the Turkmenistan border.

Little Golden Bird
This song was composed by Ustad Ghulam Hussein (1887-1967). It describes the excitement of the arrival of a new bride. The bride is welcomed by a little golden bird, the aroma of the traditional rice dish (pilau) cooking, and the cleanliness and freshness of the house.

Coo Coo Coo Maple Leaf
For centuries, this well-loved traditional chant has been enjoyed by Afghan children, particularly girls.

Little Red Bird
Composed by Ustad Ghulam Hussein, this song describes the customary pastime of Afghan children to patiently watch birds as they build their nests, as they often do, around the corners of the house windows. The children wait patiently for days, observing the egg-laying, and then excitedly await the arrival of the baby birds.

Old Man Who Braids Chains
Boys and girls enjoy singing and acting out this call-and-response chant. Children particularly enjoy imitating the sounds of the Dhol and Surnai, traditional Afghan instruments.

Song of Saalang
Afghan children love to sing about the beauty of nature. This song, arranged by Vaheed Kaacemy, describes the beautiful Saalang River Valley, located north of Kabul in the northeast region of Afghanistan, where wild flowers, birds, waterfalls, fruit trees, and berries are found in abundance. Associated with the Saalang River Valley is the famous Saalang Tunnel, a pass 2.6 km long through the Hindu Kush Mountains, connecting northern and southern Afghanistan.

Song of Spring
Composed by Ustad Ghulam Hussein, this familiar song describes spring in Afghanistan, a beautiful time of year. In this song the beauty of spring, the freshness of the grass, the blossoming of flowers, the roaring river, the chirping birds, and the ripening of fruits are all celebrated.

The Book
Composed by Vaheed Kaacemy, the intent of this song is to remind Afghan children about the importance of books. Books can bring a child great joy and satisfaction. They can be the source of many answers and can be a child's close friend.

Star
In this lovely song, the beauty of the stars in the sky and the flowers of the earth are honored. Based on a traditional Afghan melody, this song was arranged by Vaheed Kaacemy.

Afghan People
The Afghan people are proud of their country. This familiar song, composed by Ustad Ghulam Hussein, poetically describes the beauty of Afghanistan and the strength and uniqueness of the Afghan people.

Transliteration of Songs

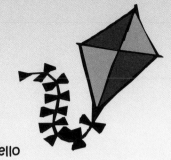

Alphabet Song

Aa Alef Bay Pay Tay Say Jeem Chay Hay Khay
Aa Alef Bay Pay Tay Say Jeem Chay Hay Khay
Aa Alef Bay Pay Tay Say Jeem Chay Hay Khay
Aa Alef Bay Pay Tay Say Jeem Chay Hay Khay

Daal Zaal Ray Zay Jhay Seen Sheen Swaat
Dwaat Toy Zoy Aine Ghine

Fay Qhaaf Kaaf Ghaaf Laam Meem Noon Wow
Fay Qhaaf Kaaf Ghaaf Laam Meem Noon Wow

Noon Wow Hay-gerdak Yaa
Noon Wow Hay-gerdak Yaa

Ali Baba

Ali Baa Baa baagh may-rowa
Dareen baagh yak bara daara
Bah bah bah mekona
Bogo dega chi daara

Ali Baa Baa baagh may-rowa
Dareen baagh yak peshak daara
Meow meow meow mekona
Bogo dega chi daara

Ali Baa Baa baagh may-rowa
Dareen baagh yak sagak daara
Ghow ghow ghow mekona
Bogo dega chi daara

Ali Baa Baa baagh may-rowa
Dareen baagh yak morghaabee daara
Qekh qekh qekh mekona
Bogo dega chi daara

Ali Baa Baa baagh may-rowa
Dareen baagh yak khargosh daara
Am am am mekona
Zeraa aawaz nadara

Hello, Hello

Salaam salaam aapa ju
Salaam salaam aata ju
Aata jo padar jaani
Aapa jo maathar jaani
Salaam salaam aapa ju
Salaam salaam aata ju

Baaba jora dost daram
Aaja jora dost daram
Baaba jo bazaar moora
Mara qet kho moobara

Salaam salaam baaba ju
Salaam salaam Aaja ju
Khowar jaana dost daram
Beraar jaana dost daram
Beraar jo har roz mara
Qet kho maktab moobara

Salaam salaam aapa ju
Salaam salaam aata ju

Bread Story

Daweedam daweedam daweedam
Saray kohay raseedam

Do taa khaanuma deedam
Yakeesh mara ow daad

Yekeesh mara naan daad
Naana khudam khordam

Owa ba zameen daadam
Zameen mara gandum daad

Ganduma ba aasya daadam
Aasya mara aard daad
Aarda ba taghar daadam
Tagaara mara khameer daad
Khameera ba naanwa daadam
Naanwa mara naan daad
Naana ba mullah daadam
Mullah mara ketaab daad
Ketaab-esha khaandam
Khudaa mara imaan daad

Polka Dot Ball

Topak-e-man khaal-khaal-eest
Gerd wa qashang gul gulest

Topak-e-man khaal-khaal-eest
Gerd wa qashang gul gulest

Zanam zameen mera baa-laa
Choon kay mey-a-nash khaleest

Zanam zameen mera baa-laa
Choon kay mey-a-nash khaleest

To-pe azizak-e-man
Bia ba peshak-e-man

To-pe azizak-e-man tu baash
Mayree baash baa tu may rum

Ah ah ah

Grandmother Swings Me

Boody boody taal raa ka
Taal dee pa me-saal raa ka

Taal dee pa me-saal raa ka
Taal kee ba zengeezuma

De-moor gheez kee tu dee-zuma
De-moor gheez kee tu dee-zuma

Gheej Gheej Don

Taam dah chemcheq seery dah
Taal bargeeny cheeny dah
Taam dah chemcheq seery dah
Taal bargeeny cheeny dah

Taal bargee a cheeq aikaan
Yow rah kay sincheq aikaan

Gheej gheej daan
Alla gheej gheej daan

Abdul Qader kamj daan
Cheeqadam pesta teergany
Aay jamalni korgany
Cheeqadam pesta teergany
Aay jamalni korgany
Aay jamal aweedah seezma

Gheej gheej daan
Ala gheej gheej daan
Abdul Qader kamj daan

Little Golden Bird

Az baalaa ow meyaa ya
Booy palow meyaa ya
Khaana ra jaaroo kunane
Aaros-e-now meyaa ya

Gunjeshkak-e-Tellaayee
Zard o safaid o siayee
Eeso ooso may pari
Khas o khashak may bari

Gunjeshkak-e-Tellaayee
Zard o safaid o siayee
Eeso ooso may pari
Khas o khashak may bari

Az baalaa ow meyaa ya
Booy palow meyaa ya
Khaana ra jaaroo kunane
Aaros-e-now meyaa ya

Gunjeshkak-e-pie goraze
Sar-e-darakht zada khaiz
Gunjeshkak-e-Tellaayee
Zard o safaid o siayee
Gunjeshkak-e-Tellaayee
Zard o safaid o siayee

Coo Coo Coo Maple Leaf

Qu Qu Qu Barg-e-Chennar
Dukhtaraa sheeshta qataar
Meecheenan daan-e-anaar

Kaash kay kaftar mayboodum
Da hawa par mayzadum
Ow-e-zamzam maykhordum
Raig-e-darya meechendum

Share guft allaa allaa
Ma guftum dard wa balaa

Little Red Bird

Ghuchi Ghuchi bahaar shud
Waqt-e-gul-e-anaar shud
Ghuchi ghuchi bahaar shud
Waqt-e-gul-anaar shud

Tukhm betay zood zood
Tukhm-a-zayray baal ko
Har waqt chucha daady
Betay yakeesha ba ma
Tukhm betay zood zood
Tukhm-a-zaray baal ko
Har waqt chucha daady
Betay yakeesha ba ma

Ghuchi Ghuchi bahaar shud
Waqt-e-gul-e-anaar shud
Ghuchi Ghuchi bahaar shud
Waqt-e-gul-e-anaar shud

Ghuchi gak hooshyaar as
Qaased-e-bahaar as
Ghuchi gak hooshyaar as
Qaased-e-bahaar as
Ghuchi Ghuci bahaar shud
Waqt-e-gul-e-anaar shud
Tukhm betay zood zood
Tukhm-a-zayray baal ko

Tukhm betay zood zood
Tukhm-a-zayray baal ko
Har waqt chucha daady
Betay yakeesha ba ma
Ghuchi ghuchi bahaar shud
Waqt-e-gul-anaar shud

Old Man Who Braids Chains

Baaba Baaba!
Balay
Zanjeer aara baafti?
Balay
Pusht-e-qala andaakhti?
Balay
Az rye-e-dol berame yaa az rye-e-surnye?
Az rye-e-surnye

Sssur sur sur
Sur sur sur
Sssur sur sur
Sur sur sur

Baaba baaba!
Balay?
Zanjeer aara baafti?
Balay
Pusht-e-qala andaakhti?
Balay
Az rye-e-dol berame yaa az rye-e-surnye?
Az rye-e-dol

Dum dum dum
Dum dum dum
Dum dum dum
Dum dum dum

Song of Saalang

Saalang koh wa darya daarah
Darya khroshaan ast
Har so gulestaan ast
Gunjeshk haa safaid wa sorkh wa zard wa sabz paran ast
Bar shaakh-saaraan ast
Maiehan naam-e-tu roshan boohad taa een jahaan ast
Taa een jahaan ast

Saalang may-wa daara rang rang tootash feraawaan ast
Darya khroshaan ast
Sheer maahi ba darya mast mastaan raqs raqsaan ast
Maahi feraawaan ast
Maiehan naam-e-tu roshan boohad taa een jahaan ast
Taa een jahaan ast

Saalang koh wa darya daarah
Darya khroshaan ast
Har so gulestaan ast
Gunjeshk haa safaid wa sorkh wa zard wa sabz paraan ast
Bar shaakh-saaraan ast
Maiehan naam-e-tu roshan boohad taa een jahaan ast
Taa een jahaan ast

Song of Spring

Mujdah kay aamad bahaar
Sabza wa gul bay shumaar
Aabay feraawaan ba baagh
Geshta rawaan har kenaar
Ghuchee wa parwaana shud
Zenda ba booy bahaar

Bulbulai-aabi kunad
Ghul-ghula dar joy-ay-baar
Karda shoogoofa ba baagh
Darakht-e-saib wa anaar
Karda shoogoofa ba baagh
Darakht-e-saib wa anaar

Bar lab-e-aab rawaan
Saaya-e-baid wa chunaar
Ko ko zanaan faakhta
Neshasta bar shaakhsaar
Ba shaakh saro beland
Naala kunad zaar zaar

Zakhaana moor wa malakh
Gashta rawaan soy-e-kaar
Tu ham bed-ow pusht-e-kaar
Aye pesar-e-hooshyaar
Tu ham bed-ow pusht-e-kaar
Aye pesar-e-hooshyaar

The Book

Man dostay-tif-lakaanam
Zeba wa khush bayaanam
Daaram sokhan feraawaan
Dar baynayseena penhaan

Begshaa tu seena am raa
Wakun khazeena am raa
Taa baa tu raaz goyam
Sad qesa baaz goyam

Man dostay-tif-lakaanam
Zeba wa khush beyaanam
Daram sokhan feraawaan
Dar baynayseena penhaan

Az qesah hye-e-shereen
Az pand hye-e-dareen
Goyam ba tu fesaana
Khuwaanam ba tu taraana

Har kas kay nukta daan shud
Zeba wa khush beyaan shud
O hamnesheen-e-man bood
Dost wa qereen-e-man bood

Man dostay-tif-lakaanam
Zeba wa khush beyaanam
Daram sokhan feraawaan
Dar baynayseena penhaan

Star

Setaara jaan setaara jaan Cheshmak Zanaan setaara jaan
Har shab ba maa qesah maygah az aasmaan setaara jaan

Gelaab wa neelofar rafeeq sosan wa nasreen mayshan
Nastran wa benafsha ham khuwaarhar yaasamin mayshan

Shab kay maysha har haft shaan az gul beta paayeen mayshan
Mayran da aasmaan baalaa setaara parween mayshan

Setaara jaan setaara jaan Cheshmak Zanaan setaara jaan
Har shab ba maa qesah maygah az aasmaan setaara jaan

Setaara tar az wara shab purkahaa dost maydaaran
Setaara Cho paana ham bara gak ha dost maydaran

Setaara hye-e-balbalee dost wa rafeeq bacha haast
Setaara parweena ham dukhtarak ha dost maydaran

Setaara jaan setaara jaan Cheshmak Zanaan setaara jaan
Har shab ba maa qesah mayga az aasmaan setaara jaan

Afghan People

Maa mardum-e-Afghaanaim
Afghaan-e-kohestaanaim

Maa mardum-e-Afghaanaim
Afghaan-e-kohestaanaim

Yak kaish wa yak aayeenaim
Yak deen wa yak armaanaim

Yak kaish wa yak aayeenaim
Yak deen wa yak armaanaim

Maa mardum-e-Afghaanaim
Afghaan-e-kohestaanaim

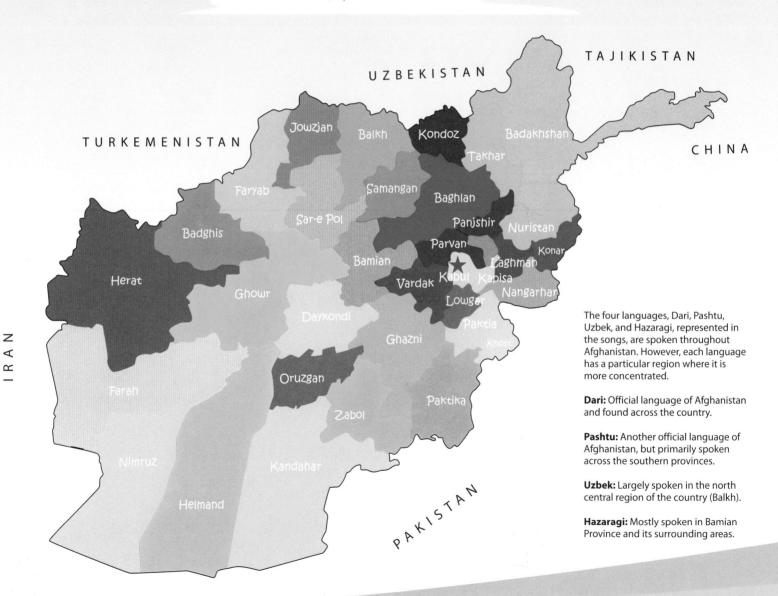

MAP OF AFGHANISTAN
with Provinces

TAJIKISTAN

UZBEKISTAN

TURKEMENISTAN

CHINA

Jowzjan
Balkh
Kondoz
Badakhshan
Takhar

Faryab
Samangan
Baghlan

Sar-e Pol
Panjshir
Nuristan

Badghis
Parvan
Konar

Bamian
Laghman

Herat
Vardak
Kabul
Kapisa

Ghowr
Lowgar
Nangarhar

Daykondi
Paktia

Ghazni
Khost

Oruzgan

Farah
Paktika

Zabol

Nimruz
Kandahar

Helmand

IRAN

PAKISTAN

The four languages, Dari, Pashtu, Uzbek, and Hazaragi, represented in the songs, are spoken throughout Afghanistan. However, each language has a particular region where it is more concentrated.

Dari: Official language of Afghanistan and found across the country.

Pashtu: Another official language of Afghanistan, but primarily spoken across the southern provinces.

Uzbek: Largely spoken in the north central region of the country (Balkh).

Hazaragi: Mostly spoken in Bamian Province and its surrounding areas.

اظهار سپاس و امتنان:
Special Thanks

In addition to all the Afghan musicians and poets from whom this collection of songs originated, we wish to thank the following:

Published by the National Geographic Society:

John M. Fahey, Jr., President and Chief Executive Officer

Gilbert M. Grosvenor, Chairman of the Board

Tim T. Kelly, President, Global Media Group

Nina D. Hoffman, Executive Vice President; President, Book Publishing Group

Staff for the Book:

Songbook Design: *Arsalan Lutfi, TriVision Studios*

Transliteration, Typesetting, and Editing: *Tabasum Lutfi, TriVision Studios*

Translation: *Shahnaz Masumi, TriVision Studios*

Music Notation: *John Roberts*

Dari Editing: *Margaret Mills*

Cover Illustration: *Susan Fisher*, with inspiration from original children's drawings

Staff for the CD:

Musical Director, Arranger, Executive Producer: *Vaheed Kaacemy*

Chief Studio Engineer: *Kushal Kana*

Children's Chorus: *Behzad Farkhari, Ghazal Farkhari, Masoud Farkhari, Khainat Hussainzada, Halina Hussainzada, Nabila Abdul, Habib Abdullah, Ramin Sultanzada, Abid Hamidi, Ramiz Hameedi, Shabir Hameedi, Noorin Band Ali, Mansour Afzali, Kaveh Wahdat, Tamineh Wahdat, and Ramez Suldeen*

Published with Financial Support from:

National Geographic Mission Programs, the Flora Family Foundation, The Ayenda Foundation, Lesley University, Richard Pascale, Jason Soules, and Celia Morris.

A Very Special Thanks to:

Arsalan Lutfi, Tabasum Lutfi, TriVision Studios, Lesley University, Lorraine Sakata, Shamim Jawad (Founder, The Ayenda Foundation), Vaheed Kaacemy and his family, Kathryn Keane, Fred Hiebert, Kathie Teter, Susan Fisher, Yasin Farkhari, Celia Morris, Jennifer Wik, Carol Chandor, Ann Carol Brown and many more family and friends who provided support and encouragement throughout this project.

31

Founded in 1888, the National Geographic Society is one of the largest nonprofit scientific and educational organizations in the world. It reaches more than 285 million people worldwide each month through its official journal, *National Geographic*, and its four other magazines; the National Geographic Channel; television documentaries; radio programs; films; books; videos and DVDs; maps; and interactive media. National Geographic has funded more than 8,000 scientific research projects and supports an education program combating geographic illiteracy.